PREFACE

In the first chapter of "Wave Of The Rock - Journey through the history of Rock" we talked about Rock, leaving aside the Biographical aspect and dedicating ourselves to the technical instrumental aspect, but also to the vocal and lyrics aspect, discovering the power of this musical genre in launching contestation messages using the power of sound and lyrics. A protest against the injustices of the world, against politics, misdeeds on the weakest, against the environment, against society in general. The lyrics also expressed the exaltation of the music that was played. That's when all this even if with great strength and determination was done with a certain control of oneself, with a right purpose, the positive part of this musical genre came out, which in my opinion is its true essence. Metal music has also been able to express these messages in a positive way. But as in Rock itself, but especially in metal music, especially in Trash Metal, when all this was expressed in an excessively angry way, sometimes out of control, instead of doing something good for the world, he reacted with depression or anger expressed in Death Metal, or in turn becoming accomplices of the bad and violent part of men, we have allied ourselves with the wrong part, often identified with the evil and dark forces. That's why the subtitle of "Wave Of The Rock 2" is "Metal Music, from contestation to occultism". Many of the songs mentioned are played with a truly impressive power and energy, now all this: it was the desire for justice, the effect of drugs or the use of occult forces ?. Also in this second chapter we will leave out the biographical aspect and we will focus on the technical-instrumental aspect of the type of sound used to express everything previously said and the type of texts. We will do all this as always by citing the most important protagonists of each Metal genre, and most famous songs, and suggestive images. There are many valuable bands that know how to make this type of music, and for each genre I have chosen those that best represent it and also those that I have listened to most to take care of the technical and instrumental aspect. So if anyone is missing, it is precisely for this reason.

TOPICS OF THE BOOK

FROM HARD ROCK TO HEAVY METAL

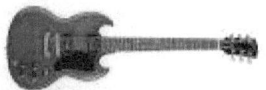

From a variation above all of the **blues**, **Rock and roll** was born mainly in the speed of the rhythm, from a harder, raw and energetic sound of *Rock and roll* with more aggressive lyrics **Rock** was born.

A fundamental feature of nascent *Rock* music was above all the lyrics, which dealt with social and protest themes against society.

A tendency to go against the current very characteristic of the style, especially in *Grunge* and *Punk Rock*, which also gave birth to the birth of many cultural movements including *Rockers*, and the *Punk culture*, which is still widespread in young people today, which they immediately stand out in their way of dressing.

What distinguishes this genre from the instrumental point of view is a sonority that sees the use mainly of the amplified electric guitar, accompanied by the electric bass and the drums, that created a hard, strong and incisive sound, referred to at the origin of the Word itself.

Several musical groups have also included the keyboard, but always in minimal part in this type of songs.

Both in England and in the US it began to appear in the early 70s, but it marked all the 80s and 90s, let's talk about **Hard Rock**. From the genres described in the previous chapters, we start to use guitars with distorted sound more and more, among the first we have seen the ***Rolling Stones***, but not only for the solos but also for the rhythm, the bass played with less notes, riffs and scales, performed only in particular points of the piece, is used to mark the rhythm of the piece often with particular effects, many times with an almost metallic sound.

From *Hard Rock* then **Heavy Metal** was born, with a louder volume, rhythm and intensity of sound, complete absence of keyboard, and the guitars that were usually two, were often both used with distortion. The boundary between *Hard rock* and *Heavy Metal* has always been thin, so much so that often the two were identified in one thing, but in *Hard Rock* you can still distinguish the origins of *Rock and Roll*, while the way to perform the song *Heavy Metal* acquires a new identity of its own.

With the birth of **Heavy Metal** the ties from the *Rock and Roll* ladders are evident, which were often used by *Hard Rock* Groups, many of whom always in love with this genre, *AC DC*, *Guns' Roses*, *Led Zeppelin* and many others.

Acid Rock is a much more noisy and energetic Psychedelic rock, **Jimi Hendrix** was neither an interpreter. This genre was also very important for the birth of **Heavy Metal**.

The **Metal sound** now has aggressive rhythms, powerful sound with an increase in the volume of the amplifiers, distortions and the bass punctuates the Rhythm with new tones and new phrasing. Many even more extreme subgenres such as **Thrash Metal**, others more melodic and commercial, were born from *Heavy Metal*.

Thrash Metal was also inspired by **Hardcore Punk** a subgenre of *punk rock*, thanks to the high speed of the rhythms and the screaming singing.

THE FIRST PROTAGONISTS

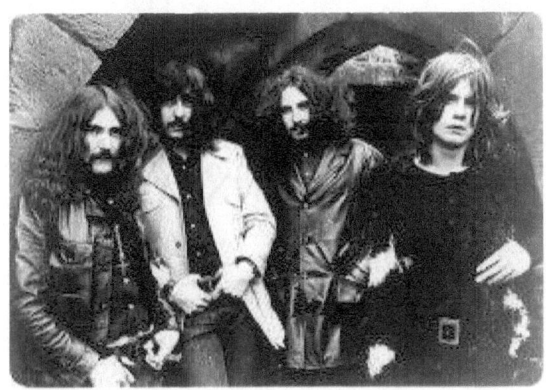

Black Sabbath, England

They were certainly among the first to play **Heavy Metal**

Before finding their ideal Sound they also played *Blues*, *Rock and Roll* and had reference to the greats of the history of Rock including the *Beatles*, **Jimi Hendrix** and others, playing their covers. In one phase they also played *Rock Progressive* and also made use of synthesizers, where they attracted criticism from their Fans.

Their great successes came when they began to use the characteristic heavy metal sound described in the previous paragraphs, with their lyrics dealing with occult, black magic and Satanism. Here too many critics were attracted, but not by their fans who were mostly young and fascinated by all this.

Hits: *Country Girl, Paranoid, Iron Man, NIB, War Pigs.*

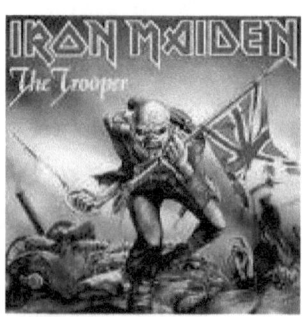

Iron Maiden (Great Britain 1975) called **Heavy Metal** Group, in fact they were. The untying of their way of playing from *Hard Rock* and its origin is evident. Rhythm changes were their characteristic, choruses with distorted chords performed without rhythm, and they performed very difficult and fast solos, with an infinite number of notes. They often performed solos on two guitars that played the exact same notes, such as the intro of Wasting Love, creating a characteristic sound of Metal.

With the song *Wasting Love* the subgenres of Heavy Metal begin to be highlighted, that is, more melodic and commercial songs.

The **Iron Maiden** texts were inspired by classical English literature, religious books, mythology, history and even TV series, and it often happened to talk about occult themes.

Other Songs to mention: ***The Trooper***, *Fear of The Dark, Two Minutes to Midnight.*

Both Black Sabbath and Iron Maiden as in the song *Fear of The Dark*, with gloomy sounds and slow rhythms that evoke decadent atmospheres, introspection and suffering, create another subgenre of the *Heavy metal*, the **Doom Metal**.

Both **Black Sabbath** and **Iron Maiden** as in the song *Fear of The Dark*, with gloomy sounds and slow rhythms that evoke decadent atmospheres, introspection and suffering, create another subgenre of the *Heavy metal*, the **Doom Metal**.

THRASH METAL AND GROOVE METAL

Thrash Metal, Subgenre of the *Heavy Metal,* reached its maximum power as regards the sonorities, making it complex and also with the appearance of Horror, also for the way to use the voice.

Metallica (Los Angeles 1981) managed to create this style with certain amps and guitars, applying a type of distortion with an atypical sound, different from that of other styles. This type of effect made the **Palm mute** technique on the guitar very powerful, which in some phases of the song was as if you heard beats and sharp sounds (hence the term *Thrash*), with this type of sound it was possible to perform great *Riff* effect, like in the song *Sad But True*.

The tracks with very fast stages had short sudden changes of rhythm and drum counter-times, especially during some types of solos.

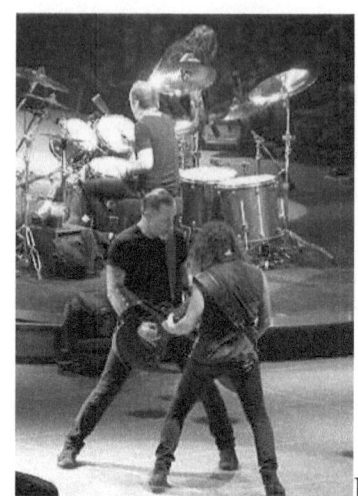 **Metallica**

As we see in the photo there was a great understanding between the singer and the guitarist, so much so that they performed some solos together and performed the same and identical notes, *creating a captivating and particular sound typical of their genre, we remember the song* **Moth Into Flame**..

They did not abandon *Heavy Metal*, in fact, they wrote many songs of this genre, and also of Soft Rock, ***Nothing Else Matters*** was an example. Other tracks ***One, Unforgiven I and II, Enter Sandman***, ***Fade to Black***.

Their texts dealt with misdeeds against humanity, throughout history towards men and towards the environment, hypocrisy of political, military and religious leaders, then anger, drugs and even the exaltation of the music they played.

Anthrax also dealt with the exaltation of their music, as in *Bring the noise* where they also expressed *Alternative Metal* collaborating with Rappers, playing *Rap Metal*, which we will discuss later.

Megadeth are one of the most famous *Thrash* bands for their protests against society, politics, environmentalism, violence, cynicism, drugs, war. The best known song is *Symphony of Destruction*, against the abuse of power by world powers.

In addition to playing *Hard Rock*, **Guns N 'Roses** played a metal with a dirtier, more raw and street sound than **Sleaze Metal.**

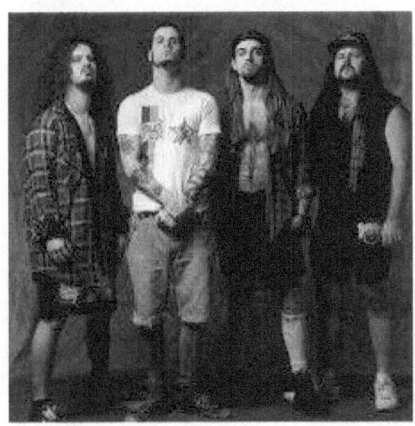 **Pantera (USA)**

Pantera appeared in the 80s and was the symbol of **Thrash Metal**, certainly for the sound, but above all for the way of using the voice of the singer **Phil Anselmo.**

The guitars fully expressed the *Thrash* style which like Metallica thanks to the use of certain amplifiers and guitars, obtained a very powerful *Palm Mute* technique that allowed the instrument to perform spectacular *Riffs*, which with the singer's voice expressed all their power . The introduction of the double bass drum in the drums also did its part, alternating very fast rhythms with stopped guitar riffs.

For this way of playing the **Groove Metal** genre was also attributed to him, and also considered the precursors of this new genre.

Pantera expressed one of the most powerful genres of Metal music both in sending the messages, but also in the sounds, which always remained listenable and engaging.

Here is one of the cases when you express yourself with excessive anger until you get out of control.

If they did not go out of control, surely the audience under the stage, pushing against each other (mosh), going wild enough to go on stage for the musicians and then throw themselves back on the crowd.

Which in their concerts happened repeatedly and done by several people at the same time.

All of this led to one of their concerts in a tragedy, when a delirious fan took the stage and shot guitarist **Dimebag Darrell.**

This news event decreed the end of the band.

Their texts dealt with Religion, death, anger and rebellion, bewilderment and disappointment from the world.

Songs: *Walk, Revolution is my name, cowboy from hell.*

GOTHIC METAL

In the previous book "Wave Of The Rock" we talked about *Gothic Rock* which was fully represented by **Evanescence.**

In their sonorities they made a lot of use of distortion in the guitar, there was no lack of keyboards and their effects, and the piano.

They often used the piano, which usually appeared when the volume of the song was decreasing, and then disappeared when the song increased in intensity again. The mix of all these instruments plus the singer's voice created the *Gothic-Dark* sounds.

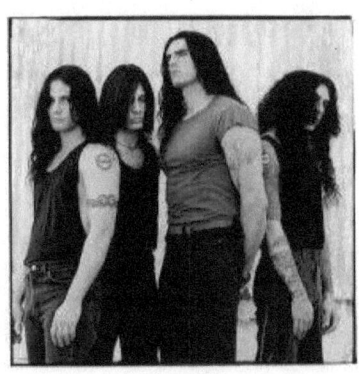
Type o Negative (USA)

The **Type O Negative** group appeared in the mid-1980s, the differences from Gothic Rock are evident in the sound, the types of effects used on the guitar, the emphasized *Palm Mute* technique, and the powerful voice of the leader **Peter Steele**.

Here too the piano is often used, the *Type or Negative* even used the harpsichord, evoking medieval atmospheres. They also have in common the changes in volume intensity of the song, which could begin by singing in a very low and faint voice, where you can barely understand the words, until you reach Screaming in some places of the song in the case of *Peter Steele*. When both the voice and the instruments dropped again in intensity, the piano or the harpsichord came out, creating the **Gothic Metal** atmosphere.

With themes of romance, death and depression, as well as the Gothic style, **Doom Metal** also played.

Among the most beautiful songs: *Black no 1, Christian Woman, Love you to Death, Everything Dies.*

Type or Negative fully represented this style, but there were also other bands that played it, **Theaters des Vampires**, lovers of horror literature and in particular vampire themes, then the Portuguese **Moonspell**, the Italian group of **Lacuna Coil** in their beginning, and others yet.

The presence of deep, depressing and intense dark atmospheres, capable of thrilling those who listen to it, highlights the union of elements present in *Gothic Rock* and the typical sounds of **Heavy Metal**.

The genus is often characterized by the alternation of ethereal female soprano and male voices, generally more aggressive that alternate or overlap.

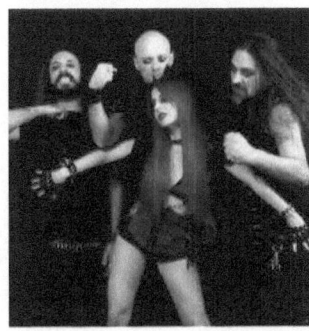 **Theatre Des Vampires**

As in the song *Angel Of Lust* by **Theater Des Vampires** group Italino Gothic Metal.

The themes of their texts are intuitive by their name, they are mostly vampire tales, also highlighted by the scenes of their videos.

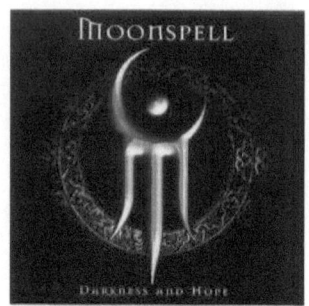

Video clip is also very important in this musical genre, in making everything even more intense and fascinating. We saw it for *Theater Des Vampires*, and it was like that for *Type O Negative* too.

The **Moonspell** in the song *Nocturna* are very good with their sounds and the setting of the video, to evoke particular dark atmospheres of the night.

DEATH METAL

Heavy Metal subgenre spread in the late 80's in the (USA). Despite being an extreme genre therefore with a niche audience, especially for the topics covered, the criticism was not excessively harsh and managed to find ample space in North America and Europe.

The topics covered are Pain, Death and Suffering, which are sometimes narrated in a comical or satirical way, trying to exorcise or play down the harshness of the contents.

One of the inspiring groups were the **Slayer**,

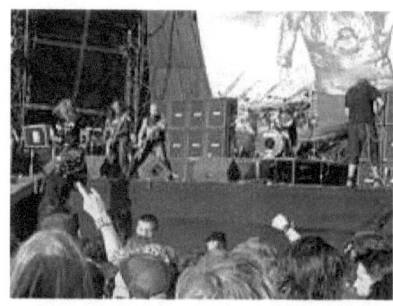 **Slayer, Los Angeles (USA)**

Their texts were about Satanism, Nazism, war, death, so they become part of two genres, both **Death Metal**, but 23 also the

Black Metal that we will see later.

More than from the *Heavy metal*, this genre derives from the *Thrash Metal* played by the **Slayer**, when they began to play at a faster and pressing pace.

Their successes include ***Rainig Blood, Seasons in the Abyss, Skeletons Of Society.***

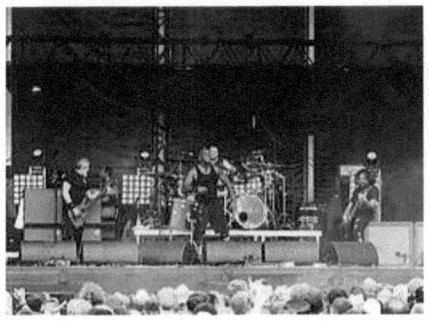

The **Sepultura** Brazilians we see in the photo also played **Death Metal** which mixed with *Alternative Metal* and *Groove* making it creative and listenable. One of their hits was ***Territory***.

Arch Enemy played a more melodic *Death Metal* despite the singer's powerful scream voice, as in the song ***The Eagle flies alone.***

Other bands that played it: **Morbid Angel, At the gates.**

In the most extreme versions, ***Death Metal*** from my point of view is almost unheard from the technical point of view of sound, except in some parts of the song.

The drums become very fast and with a pounding rhythm, widely using the distorted guitar, and a very screaming voice.

In this type of songs rather than the melody, the message you want to send to the fans (fans) is highlighted, moreover in a rather violent way.

BLACK METAL

It appears in the first half of the 80s and has origin in northern Europe Norway, Sweden and Finland. *Along with Death and one of the most extreme genres of Metal music.*

The topics covered, Satanism, Anti-Christianity, paganism. More than for the musical quality, this type of music has obtained media coverage for the crime stories that involved the protagonists of the bands (suicides, vandalisms, murders).

As in the most extreme versions of *Death*, even **Black Metal** makes use of the double drum case, extremely distorted and violent sound, *Scream* voice, with little attention to the melodic aspect, except for some parts of the song, where acoustic guitar arpeggios, evoke ancestral atmospheres inspired by northern European folk rock, as in many song of **Mayhem.**

Similar to Death also with regard to the themes of some texts such as nihilism, misanthropy, death, but in Death the rhythms are more frequent.

Among the best known *Black Metal* bands: ***Venom, Mayhem, Immortal.*** **Venom** (Great Britain) wrote a song dedicated to this extreme genre, ***Black Metal.***

Immortal's *All Shall Fell* is a song that fully represents this genre, the most aggressive parts of the song, at a certain point are interrupted by arpeggiated guitar phases, which with particular effects evoke suggestive and surreal atmospheres.

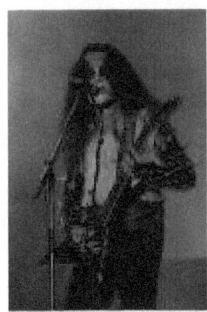

Chitarrista Immortal

As in the *All Shall Fell* video, the protagonists of **Black Metal** were often dressed and made up in a very particular way, becoming part of the **Glam Metal**, which we will discuss later.

Black Metal began to be more valued from a technical and sound point of view, when synthesizers and symphonic instruments were introduced. It was one of the many facets of this genre, where the sinister sound evoking surreal

29

atmospheres, and the themes described at the beginning of the chapter, are the protagonists.

The *Scream* voice is inevitable. This genre is also characterized by a more acute distorting effect on the guitar than the other Metal genres.

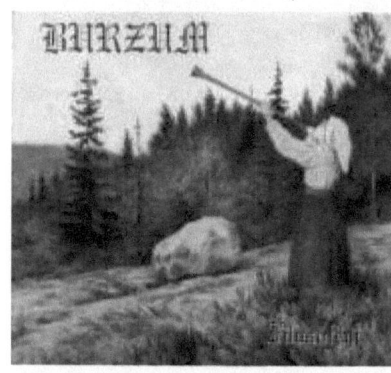 **Burzum Album Cover**

All this is found in many of **Burzum**'s songs, where in some songs not even the distorted sound of the guitar appears. Where instead it is present in the song *Lost Wisdom.*

Those who best expressed this particular musical genre were the Norwegian Bands: **Immortal, Mayhem, Burzum**.

POWER METAL

It is inspired by *Heavy Metal* and *Thrash Metal*, characterized by long-lasting songs, and the use of the keyboard for most bands, especially Scandinavian.

Present in the USA with **Iced Earth**, in Europe with **Helloween, Gamma Ray**

The main feature of this subgenre are the themes: mythology, fantasy, science fiction and metaphysics; But also the way of playing the guitar above all, with a more acute Distortion effect, scales of different solos, and chords often played without rhythm, letting the distortion vent until the chord or the new rhythm is changed Even the voice with a more acute, classic sound of Heavy metal.

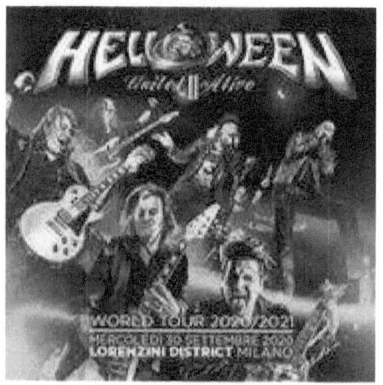

As in *I Want Out song* of the *Halloween*, sound similar to that of *Fear The Dark by* Iron Maiden, in fact, the latter also played this genre.

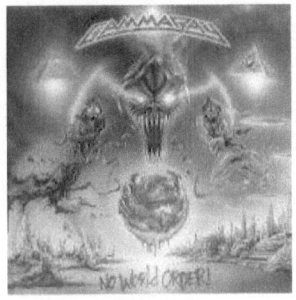

The Germans **Gamma Ray** with - *No World Order* highlight the long duration of this genre of **51 minutes.**

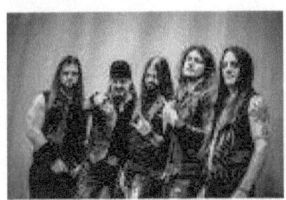**Ice The Earth**

Iced Earth unites the typical sounds of *Heavy Metal* and *Thtash Metal* with the themes of **Power**, as in the songs of the *Incorructible* album.

ALTERNATIVE METAL

It is a subgenre of *Heavy Metal* mixed with *Alternative Rock* that we talked about extensively in the previous book. This mixture leads to a fairly clear detachment from classic *Heavy metal*, but not as evident as when *Heavy metal* merges with other very different genres such as *Rap*, which we will discuss in the penultimate chapter.

Almost All the groups that mainly played Thrash Metal that we saw in the first chapters, or for a variation of the rhythms and timbres of the sound, or for mixes with other genres, also played **Alternative Metal.**

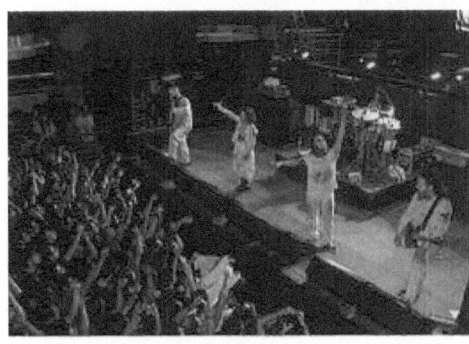 **Lacuna Coil (Italia)**

Lacuna Coil began with a *Gothic Rock* sound, but slowly found their identity, creating a personal style, also using two voices, one male and one female.

However, they did not abandon the dark themes of the early *Gothic* era. Because of their way of dressing, they too became part of **Glam Metal.**

Songs to mention: ***Trip in the darkness, Layers of time*** and a cover that has been very successful, that of ***Enjoy The Silence*** by ***Depeche mode.***

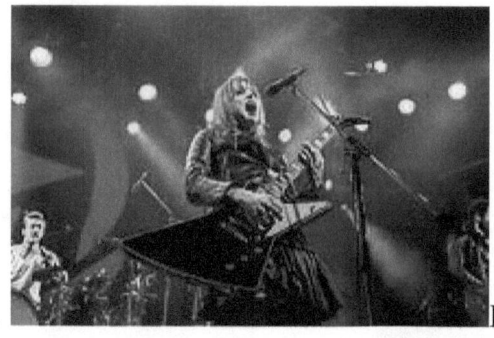
Halestorm, Pennsylvania.

Halestorm, Band on the border between *Hard Rock* and *Heavy Metal*, in many songs expressed an **Alternative Metal**.

The sounds and voice of the guitarist singer **Lzzy Ale** is very powerful, who in some stages of the songs screamed, but always with a clean voice and without losing intonation. Among their successes: *I miss the misery, Mayhem, I am the fire*,

Both **Lacuna Coil** and **Halestorm** in many of their songs have distinguished themselves for spectacular guitar *Riffs*.

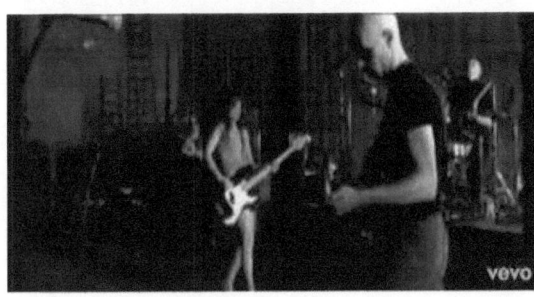 **A Perfect Circle**

At **Perfect Circle** they also played *Alternative Metal* from an *Alternative Rock* inspiration, another of the genres that the band played.

In one of their phases they wrote texts against the war. This is also a very active group even after 2000 writing songs until a few years ago. S

ongs: *Judith, Week and Powerless, Disillusioned, The Outsider.*

Other *Alternative Metal* Bands: **Helmet, Linkin Park, Ministry.**

In this chapter we can see (in *Alternative Metal*, but also in other Metal genres), the tendency or the need for a female component in the bands, or for the voice, or in the case of **A Perfect Circle** in the use of an instrument, the bass.

PROGRESSIVE METAL

This too is a subgenre of *Heavy metal* born in the late 1980s. It combines the aggressiveness and the typical volume of *Heavy Metal* with the complexity and classic ambitions of *Progressive Rock*.

The *Progressive* style we talked about in the first book of "Wave Of The Rock" is characterized by long-lasting songs and with the addition of orchestral instruments, transverse flutes, strings, and even the keyboards with its effects. The style mixed with rock as *Pink Floyd* and *Genesis* did resulted in *Rock Progressive*.

When musical groups such as **Dream Theater, Symphony X, Queensryche,** mixed it with metal music in particular *Heavy Metal*, they obtained the **Progressive Metal** style.

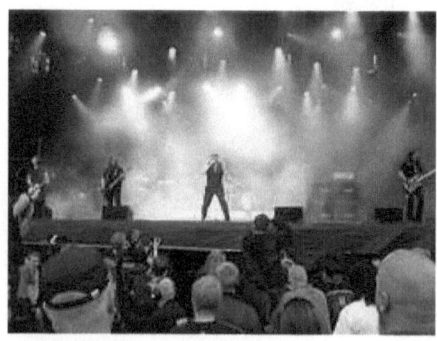

Queensryche, Seattle

Among their most beautiful songs: *Empire*, which reaches 5 minutes, in *Best I can*, you can notice the progressive characteristics of the band.

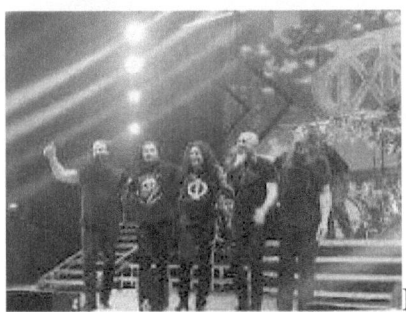

Dream Theater

One of the best known songs is *Another Day* where the mix with Heavy Metal is evident, the piano and the virtuosity of the symphonic instrument at the end of the song are inevitable.

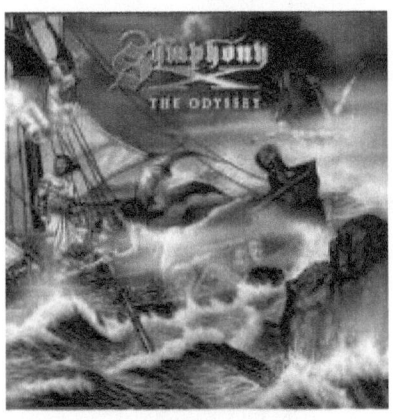

Cover of the Album *"The Odyssey"* **Symphony X**

In the song that gives title to this album *The Odyssey* there are *Heavy Metal* sounds mixed with real symphonic instruments, generated by electronic keyboards, or samplers, especially at the beginning. The piece has various phases, in some parts there are guitar arpeggios that evoke the more melodic aspect of Heavy Metal, in other phases the classic one. With a duration of 24.14 minutes, this is one of the songs that fully represents the style of this chapter.

ELECTRONICORE AND INDUSTRIAL METAL

The *hardcore punk* subgenre of *punk rock* was very important for the birth of **Thras Metal**, as we saw in previous chapters.

When the Synthesizer, the electronic drums, and technological equipment capable of modifying the songs with particular effects or introducing them are added to the *Hardcore Punk* characterized by fast rhythms, guitar distortion, screamed voice, a sort of **Electronic Metal** is born called more precisely **Electronicore,** which spread to the United States and Great Britain.

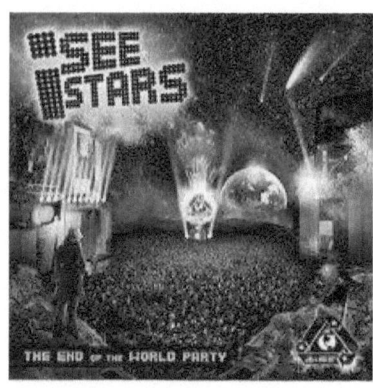 **I See Stars (USA)**

Often in this type of songs, in addition to the obvious effects electronic mixed with Metal sounds, the voice alternated with Scream and clean and melodic phases.

Band: **I See Stars, Sky etas airplane, Breathe Carolina, Issues, Crossfaith.**

Songs: *Calm now* (I See Stras), *Giants in the Ocean* (Sky eats airplane), *Sellouts* (Breathe Carolina).

Industrial Metal is very similar, But it does not have the aggressiveness of the Electronicore. Some parts of the songs are played with classic metal instruments, electric guitar, bass and drums, with the addition of electronic drums, samplers, synthesizers, keyboards. The vocal style is usually used cleanly, except for some parts of the song with a Scream voice, sometimes created or transformed by electronics.

Groups: **Ministry, Nine Inch Nails, Fear Factor.**

Songs : *Archetype* (Fear Factor), *N.W.O.* (Ministry), *Wish* (Nine Inch Nails**).**

The more hybrid and unpredictable the result of the mix, the more we move towards an *experimental Metal* or **Avant-Garde Metal.**

OTHER TYPES OF METAL MUSIC

Metal Music deriving from *Heavy Metal* which in turn comes from **Rock,** since the instruments used are the same, retains the characteristic of Mixing, that is, the ease of mixing with other musical genres.

This favored the birth of other subgenres:

Dance Metal, Rap Metal, Funk Metal, Folk Metal, Pop Metal or Hair Metal etc ... all born from the fusion of *Heavy Metal* and its characteristics with Music Dance, Rap, Funky, folk, Pop etc...

This type of mix is also called **Nu Metal**, which becomes even more innovative when the electronic sounds typical of Industrial Metal are also present in the mix.

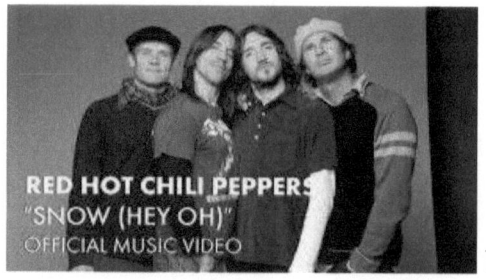 USA

Precursors of this musical genre, the **Red Hot Chili Peppers,** Which we described in the first book when they introduced the typical *Funk* rhythms to the sound of Rock, and sometimes the outburst of their refrains came out by Ripping the lyrics.

When all this is mixed with harder and more aggressive sounds (typical of the *Heavy Metal*), the musical genres described at the beginning of this chapter come out.

Anthrax, to find new audiences and a wider success by incorporating in the band of Rapper, they were also precursors, in particular of *Rap Metal;*

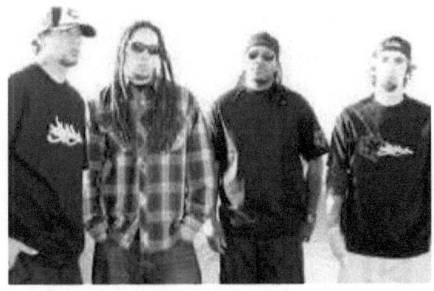 **P.O.D.**

Youth of the Nation a beautiful piece by P.O.D., a slightly more melodic *Rap Metal*, but they also wrote many other songs in this style, where the distorted guitar is more evident.

49

Among the major exponents of *Nu-Metal* the **Korn**, still in business, who play this genre with great energy and power.

Other Band: **Linkin Park, Primus, Fishbon, Living Colour.**

The **Linkin Park** we mentioned in the previous book (Wave Of The Rock) were one of the most versatile bands, which spanned multiple genres in Rock-Metal music.

We have already talked about the **Doom Metal** and **Groove Metal** obtained not with mixes, but with variations in rhythms, in the first chapters.

The term **Glam** that comes from **Glamor** (*Charm*), is not referred to the sound, but to the way of dressing and moving on the stage of the protagonists. The band as well as playing their own genre, when they began to dress in a strange way and with attitudes on the stage to amaze and impress the audience, they also became part of the **Glam Metal** genre.

Slipknot Band *Nu-Metal* but incorporating *Death Metal*, *Trash Metal* and *Groove*, for their way of dressing and acting on stage, go beyond *Glam*, let's talk about ***Shock Rock*** or ***Shock Metal.***

METAL MUISC TODAY

In the previous chapter we talked about **Linkin Park**, a band that in the field of Rock and Metal music wrote songs of all kinds, playing *Alternative Rock, Alternative Metal, Nu-Metal, Rap Metal*, also *Dance Metal*, writing songs until a few years ago .

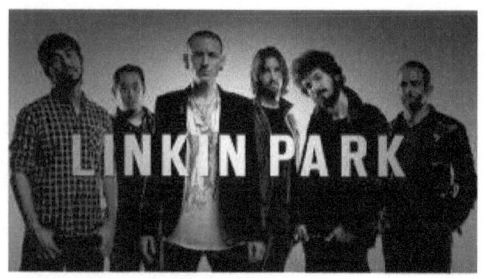

Precisely for this reason, today I am at the top of the ranking of visits (about 1 billion) through the various Apps and YT (Stream) with many songs: The most famous ***In The End***, then gradually all the other ***One Step Closer, Numb, What I made, crawling, glass castle*** etc ...

Then band like: **Shinedown, A day to remember, Alice in Chains** and others, with hundreds of millions of views.

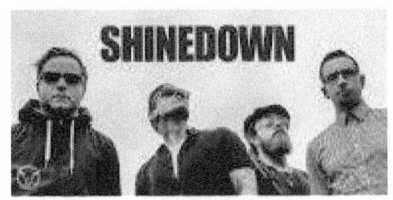

Sound The Madness, How Did you love among the songs of **Shinedown**, a group that is continuing to write songs, very active from 2000 until today.

Taking the statistical data of the most listened to in the first places there are the bands mentioned in this chapter, all this possible with a compromise between *Metal* and *Alternative Rock* whose result is **Alternative Metal**.

There are also many recent albums by Extreme Metal, like *Black* and *Death Metal*, especially those of new debut bands.

Game Zero is one recent Italian heavy metal band (2013) very talented, who plays a more modern Metal, with very interesting *Riffs* and melodies. Among the topics covered, the War.

Then there are the songs of the historical bands mentioned in this book, the **"Unforgettable"**. That often, *only with the first three most famous songs*, exceed *one billion views*.

TECHNICAL TERMS OF ROCK AND METAL

Here are the technical terms used in the previous book which fits perfectly with this by adding new terms used in Metal music, in order to make them complete for this book. This is to facilitate and make reading easier even for non-musicians:

Amplifier: Instrument that through speakers amplifies and enhances the sound produced by a musical instrument.

Bottleneck: it is a 5-7 cm hollow cylinder to be inserted on the finger and which, sliding on the guitar strings, gives them a particular sound, used above all in genres such as country and blues.

Electric guitar: It is a type of guitar in which the vibration of the metal strings is detected by one or more pick-ups; the signal is then picked up at the output and conveyed to an amplifier so that the sound is audible.

Folk guitar: It is an acoustic guitar, that is, that the sound is reproduced by the vibrations of the soundboard. Unlike the classical guitar, it is designed to accommodate metal strings instead of nylon strings.

All this causes a different sound, used in the execution of pieces of modern music, blues, folk, rock and, in general, of light music. With the use of external pick-ups, or if already set up, the sound can become even louder through the connection to amplifiers.

Chorus: Effect for guitars that gives the instrument more body in the sound. It is obtained by recording the sound of the guitar itself, and then mixing it with the original with a minimum delay, creating a sound similar to that of a chorus of multiple guitars.

Deley: Effect for guitar or other instruments that serves to record the sound and reproduce it continuously with a certain delay, obtaining an echo of the sound until it fades. The delay can be regulated by special pedals.

Distortion: Effect for electric guitar that changes its timbre, the dynamics is the duration of the sound, making it similar to that of an amplifier pushed beyond its possibilities, which saturates, distorts the sound, giving it the typical characteristics of rock music. This effect can be obtained with a special pedal, where you can adjust the volume, and more.

Echo: Ancient effect that Pink Floyd used to give more body and a characteristic sound to keyboards.

Flanger: Guitar effect that in addition to being able to create Chorus and Deley, can reproduce various noises almost similar to the noise of a Jet taking off.

Palm Mute: Guitar technique which consists in damping the sound with the palm of the right hand, resting it lightly on the strings. The same hand that pinches the string, obtaining a characteristic and particular sound.

Riff: In the guitar it is meant a particular musical passage consisting of a succession of notes that frequently occurs within the piece (often also at the beginning), characterizing it. The Riff is usually not very long and gives a strong expressiveness to the song. Sometimes it can be used as an accompaniment for most of its duration.

Reverb: It is similar to the deley, only while in the deley the echo effect is reproduced with a certain delay, we speak of several seconds, the reverberation reproduces the sound after a delay of fractions of a second making it very different from the first.

Pick-up: Electric device that allows you to transform the vibrations of the guitar strings into electrical impulses so that they can be transmitted to the amplifier to enhance its sound.

Sampler: instrument sampler that can be connected to a midi keyboard (or other electronic devices) so that you can play with many other types of musical instruments. There are also software now that does this on the computer.

Scream: used mainly in black metal, it is a screamed voice similar to an exasperated scream. Also this technique can be performed by dirtying the sound (and therefore scratching on the vocal cords) or keeping it as clean as possible.

Synthesizer: Very complex electronic instrument that is capable of generating, sampling and reproducing the sounds of any instrument, noises, and any other effects. It can be used during a concert by musicians to let that type of sound enter at the set time, automatically or under someone's command.

Slide: Guitar technique that consists of changing notes or chords by sliding your fingers on the keyboard.

String: Effect used mainly on keyboards to create a background for music, but also for other. Playing a musical chord, the String imitates a set of bowed instruments, violins, violas, cellos etc ...

Tapping: it is a guitar technique that allows you to play notes directly on the fretboard without plucking the strings, using the fingers of the right or left hand, or simultaneously to be able to perform even more complex sounds and scales.

Wah-wah: Musical effect widely used on guitars giving it a sound similar to a cry or a meow.

GLOSSARY OF ARTISTS AND MUSICAL GENRES:

Anthrax: Trash Metal, Alternative Metal (15,49);

A Perfect Circle: Alternative Metal (37,38);

Arch Enemy: Death Metal (25);

At the gates: Death Metal (26);

Black Sabbath: Heavy Metal (9,10,11);

Breathe Carolina: Electronicore (45);

Burzum: Black Metal (30);

Crossfaith: Electronicore (45);

Dream Theater: Progressive Metal (40,41);

Evanescence: Gothic Rock, Dark Rock (19);

Fear Factor: Industrial Metal (45);

Fishbon: Nu-Metal (50);

Gamma Ray: Power Metal (32);

Guns N' Roses: Hard Rock, Heavy Metal, Sleaze Metal (15);

Iced Earth: Power Metal (32,33);

Immortal: Black Metal, Glam Metal (29,30);

Iron Maiden: Heavy Metal (10,11,33);

I See Stars: Electronicore (44,45);

Issues: Electronicore (45);

Jimi Hendrix: Rock, Rock Psichedelico, Acid Rock (7,9);

Halestorm : Alternative Metal, Heavy Metal, Hard Rock (36,37);

Helmet: Alternative Metal (38);

Helloween: Power Metal (32,33);

Korn: Nu Metal, Alternative Metal, Rap Metal (50);

Lacuna Coil: Gothic Metal, Alternative Metal, Glam metal (20,35,37);

Linkin Park: Rock Elettronico; Rap e Dance Metal, Alternative Metal, Nu-Metal (38,50,52);

Living Colour: Nu-Metal (50);

Mayhem: Black Metal (28,30);

Megadeth: Trash Metal (15);

Metallica: Heavy Metal, Trash Metal (13,14,16);

Ministry: Alternative Metal, Industrial Metal (38,45);

Morbid Angel: Death Metal (26);

Moonspell: Gothic Metal (20,22);

Nine Inch Nails: Industrial Metal (45);

Pantera: Thrash Metal, Groove Metal (15,16,17);

Primus: Nu-Metal (50);

Queensryche: Progressive Metal (40);

Red Hot Chili Peppers: Rock Altern., Funk Rock, Rap Rock (48,49);

Sepultura: Thrash Metal, Death Metal (25);

Sky etas airplane: Electronicore (45);

Slipknot: Nu Metal, Alternative Metal, Death Metal, Rap Metal (50);

Symphony X: Progressive Metal (41,42);

Slayer: Thrash Metal, Death Metal (24,25);

Theatres Des Vampires: Gothic Metal (20,21);

Type O Negative: Gothic Metal (19,20,22);

Venom: Black Metal, Thrash Metal (28);

CONSIDERATION

As regards the Metal texts there is an important consideration to make; Many groups of this musical genre deal with **occult and obscure themes**, but this does not mean that they must necessarily be sorcerers or devil worshipers. You simply face these issues to explore and tell them from your point of view.

This is very likely for *Heavy Metal* Bands and *Thrash Metal* too. In fact, many of the protagonists confirmed that they have touched certain subjects without being Satanists, but that being considered in this way has helped them, because it has increased their charm and mystery by making them sell even more records.

Different is the case of *Black Metal* and *Death Metal* where many bands express certain topics with great strength, power and conviction, especially for the use of the voice, but also in sinister sounds.

It is up to fans, especially teenagers, to be able to choose the type of music to listen to, so that they are not negatively influenced by putting wrong beliefs in their heads.

That's why, in my opinion, not all metal music, but for particular subgenres a great critical sense is needed to listen to it.

Conclusions and Thanks

Initially the idea was to write an E-book, not too long and flowing, without prevaricating too much. This was the case, but during the drafting we arrived at a number of pages suitable for paper too. So it is available both as an E-Book and as a paper book. This book is completed and fits perfectly with the first version of "Wave Of The Rock" If you buy them both "Wave Of The Rock" and "Wave Of The Rock 2" You will have the whole history of rock from its birth until to get to the more classic Metal genres such as Heavy Metal, more extreme, alternative, and innovative (Nu-Metal and Avant-Garde Metal).

I was able to write this book thanks to the study of guitar and piano, so thanks to the teachers. To the friends who made up the various bands I was part of, which allowed me to enrich the experience on my instruments, and at the same time make me know others, the bass, the drums etc.

Thanks to all fellow guitarists, singers and musicians who have not been part of my bands, from whom I have always learned new things. Especially from those who have played genres other than mine, letting me know about instruments and dynamics, referring to *Metal* music in particular.

Thanks to the *Web* and *Wikipedia* inexhaustible sources of information that have allowed me to perfect beauty to the full, enriching it with many more details.

Finally thanks to the protagonists of this book, the Singers and the Bands, which I was able to study also thanks to the various concerts seen live and in the videos.

INDEX OF TOPICS

Written By **Salvatore Bellassai** nell'anno 2020 ;

*****

In the e-book format, use the document search box to find any topic, for example a singer, a group, a musical genre, a technical term etc...

By the same Author:

Wave Of The Rock (Journey through the History of Rock);